Yesterday's Tallahassee

OTHER VOLUMES IN

Seemann's Historic Cities Series

Seemann's Historic Cities Series No. 7

Yesterday's

TALLAHASSEE

By Hampton Dunn

E. A. Seemann Publishing, Inc.
Miami, Florida

The photographs in the volume stem from various sources, the most important one being the Florida State Photographic Archives in the Strozier Library at Florida State University in Tallahassee. All photographs without any source identification were obtained from this source. Other sources are identified in parentheses at the end of each caption. The abbreviations stand for the following:

LC   Library of Congress, Washington, D.C.
Johnson   Malcolm B. Johnson, Tallahassee, Florida
Dunn   Hampton Dunn, Tampa, Florida

To

Malcolm B. Johnson

the erudite editor of the *Tallahassee Democrat*

my friend and colleague in the journalism field for 35 years, scholar of Florida history and enthusiastic booster of his "home town" of Tallahassee.

Contents

THE TALLAHASSEE HILL COUNTRY in a map of 1898

Foreword

TALLAHASSEANS want other Floridians to recognize their state capital as every citizen's other home. Certainly, I feel that it is my other home town. For twenty-five years or more, it has been my thrill to visit frequently the seat of government, first as a political writer for the old *Tampa Daily Times,* later as a political commentator for Miami television station WCKT-TV, then in more recent years as a representative of the Peninsula Motor Club (AAA). Tallahasseé grows on you and you find yourself wanting to spend more time there.

It was an honor to be selected as a Charter Trustee of the Historic Tallahassee Preservation Board, a statewide agency, several years ago and to have a part in launching a far-reaching historic restoration and preservation effort in one of the most historic of Florida cities.

In 1974, Tallahassee is celebrating its 150th birthday anniversary, and all Floridians join in marking this significant milestone of their other home town.

As with all my other books, I could not have put them together without the valuable aid and assistance of many persons. Everyone in Tallahassee I have contacted has been most gracious and helpful.

Malcom B. Johnson, editor of the *Tallahassee Democrat* was the source of great strength and wisdom as I consulted with him on the publication of *Yesterday's Tallahassee.* In addition to giving me much background material on his home town, he turned up numerous precious photographs to round out the contents of this book.

Mrs. Joan Morris, the astute director of the State Archives in the Robert Manning Strozier Library at Florida State University, likewise was a tremendous contributor. She gladly shared with me the unique collection of Floridiana in the library, gave me a lot of useful information and advice, plus a great deal of encouragement to go ahead. Her husband, Allen Morris, Clerk of the House of Representatives and compiler of the *Florida Handbook,* also aided me in several ways. He's a friend of long-standing, back when we both were newspapermen covering the State Capitol.

The vivacious Mrs. Nancy Dodson, director of the Historic Tallahassee Preservation Board, came through with many pictures as well as ideas and words of encouragement.

The Library of Congress provided those magnificent drawings of Tallahasse in the 1830s by the French artist Count de Castelnau.

Again I am indebted to the Burgert Brothers collection for many Tallahassee scenes. This group of negatives was made available to me by Henry Cox of Tampa Photo Supply, and have provided the nucleus for several other of my "Yesterday" books.

Spring 1974   HAMPTON DUNN

The Capital in the Wilderness

TALLAHASSEE was here and had a name long before the white man came along and "discovered" it.

The Indians founded the community, developed it, deserted it, and other Indians started referring to the area as "old town" or "old fields." This was Apalachee Country, originally settled by the Apalachees, who no longer exist. The Creeks and the Seminoles came along later.

A gazeteer of Indian names reports that the name Tallahassee was translated from the Creek *Talwa* = town, and *Ahassee* = old, meaning "Old Town." Apparently the Indians came and went during their occupation of the region and referred to the site by that name.

Credit for formally naming Tallahassee when it became the state capitol in the 1820s goes to Miss Octavia Walton, daughter of Col. George Walton, Territorial Secretary and son of a signer of the Declaration of Independence. She lived in Pensacola at the time.

The Big Bend of Florida, as it now is referred to, attracted some of the earliest of the Spanish *conquistadores* in their explorations of the North American continent.

There is suspicion that Ponce de Leon himself came this way on his first voyage when he discovered Florida in 1513; some historians say Ponce went out as far as Pensacola Bay. Regardless, the county of which Tallahassee is the county seat, bears since its establishment in December 29, 1824, the name Leon. It was named for Juan Ponce de Leon, who had named Florida.

Next to climb the hills and tramp through the wilderness of this section was Panfilo de Narvaez, the swashbuckling, red-headed, one-eyed Spaniard, who entered the state at Tampa Bay in April, 1528. He had ordered his ships to

[11]

rendezvous with him in north Florida, presumably at St. Marks, just south of Tallahassee, while he led a party of men and horses overland searching for gold and silver he believed to be there. When he finally wound up in Tallahassee late in June, the entire troop was exhausted and hungry.

The Narvaez explorers found no food, and when they went to the appointed place of rendezvous with their ships carrying supplies, alas, there were no ships. Whereupon Narvaez and his men set about building some ships with which to escape. The hides of horses and palmetto wood were fashioned into ship coverings, and belt buckles and sword handles were made into winches and crude nails. Finally, five vessels were completed, and the 242 men jammed into them. Most were lost in storms in the Gulf of Mexico, but one reached the coast of Texas, from whence the survivors found their way to Mexico City. All this was taking place here in Florida nearly a century before the *Mayflower* landed at Plymouth Rock.

Next important visitor to these parts was the dashing Spanish explorer, Hernando de Soto. He and his expedition had landed at Tampa Bay in May of 1539. They started their search for gold and other treasures, up through Tampa, over to Ocala, up to Lake City, and westward to Tallahassee.

The DeSoto invaders had been under heavy attack by the Indians most of the way. Finally, they arrived in the Apalachee Province in October, and pitched camp for the winter, on the banks of beautiful Lake Jackson. The site they used is known as the Lake Jackson Mound Complex, now an undeveloped State park.

The *conquistador* brought with him a dozen or more priests, and so it is believed that the first celebration of Christmas in the present United States took place right here in Tallahassee on December 25 of 1539. Christ's Mass, the feast of the Nativity of our Lord, most certainly was said; the priests would certainly have seen to it that religious festivals were celebrated.

DeSoto bade goodbye to Tallahassee on March 3, 1540, and headed out on his ill-fated journey through the Southeast, which ended with his demise on the banks of the Mississippi River.

During the succeeding century, Spanish explorers and colonists based at St. Augustine became familiar with this Apalachee country, according to the scholarly researcher Malcolm B. Johnson, present-day editor of the *Tallahassee Democrat*.

Johnson relates that in 1639, with encouragement from the agriculturally inclined Apalachees, the Spanish set up a string of missions through this area for the combined purpose of Christianizing the Indians while protecting them from more warlike tribes to the north. In exchange, the Spanish took grain and foodstuffs back to the garrison at Saint Augustine.

This Spanish-Indian commerce flourished for 65 years, until Col. James Moore of South Carolina led a few Englishmen and a horde of Cherokees on raids into Spanish middle Florida in 1704. They destroyed all the mission

FRANCIS, COMTE DE CASTELNAU, a French traveler and artist, came to the Territory of Florida in the winter of 1837-38. He left for posterity a number of historical drawings of Tallahassee and its surroundings, published originally in 1842 in his *Vues et Souvenirs de l'Amerique du Nord*. A plantation on Lake Jackson (with a rail fence typical for the period) is shown above, and a plantation on Lake Lafayette (with log cabin and rail fence) below. (LC)

FOUR SCENES from Count de Castelnau's book showing (*above left*) an Indian village at Appalachicola; a scene on the Appalachicola River (*above right*); an arsenal (*below right*); and the Railroad Station at Tallahassee (*below left*). (LC).

forts, burned the Indian villages, slaughtered most of the men and all but depopulated the area by taking the women and children back with them into slavery.

For another century, the Apalachee country remained a comparative wilderness through which Spanish officers and soldiers passed occasionally, traveling from St. Augustine to Pensacola. It was inhabited by peaceful, agricultural Indians. They welcomed, even petitioned, Spanish protection from more warlike tribes to the north. Consequently, late in the first half of the seventeenth century, the Spanish established a chain of mission-forts in the present Tallahassee area. Christian missionaries converted Indians who tilled the fields and sent food to the garrison at Saint Augustine.

This commerce of more than fifty years ago ended abruptly in January, 1904 when Col. James Moore of South Carolina led a force of a few white men and a thousand Georgia Indians on a raid. They burned the forts and depopulated Apalachee by slaughtering the native Indians or taking them north into slavery. Apalachee again lapsed into more than a century of wilderness—marked on the map only by the deserted villages which were to give the capital its name—Tallahassee.

Seminoles, a tribe of Indians taking refuge from American efforts to resettle them westward, moved in during this period and supposedly were harboring runaway slaves from nearby Georgia, one of the original thirteen states of the union. Whereupon Andrew Jackson, the fearless Indian fighter and American soldier, rushed here in 1818 to put down the Seminoles, and burn their villages.

General Jackson became Florida's first American governor when the peninsula was taken in as a territory in 1821. There really were only two prospering settlements in the entire territory—Pensacola and Saint Augustine. The Spanish had divided the area into East Florida and West Florida with those early cities as the seats of government. Under American government, these provinces became counties—Escambia and Saint Johns—separated by the Suwannee River.

Geography became important in the rule over the far-flung wilderness territory. The first Territorial Legislative Council met in Pensacola. It was due to convene June 10, but it was not until July 22 that a quorum arrived. Delegates from Saint Augustine had to make the long, treacherous voyage around the Florida keys. One delegate drowned at sea, and some delegates never showed up. The same hardships had to be endured the next year, 1823, when the Council convened in Saint Augustine.

So it was decided to find a central location for the capital. Gov. William P. DuVal named two Commissioners—John Lee Williams of Pensacola and Dr. William H. Simmons of Saint Augustine. It was their duty to find and select a site for the capital. Simmons set out by horseback from Saint Augustine, Williams by boat from Pensacola. They were to meet at Saint Marks, but

MANSIONS began to dot the countryside shortly after Tallahassee was founded in 1824. One of the first under construction was "The Grove," at North Adams and First Avenue. It was built by Gen. Richard Keith Call, who was friend, confidante, and top aide to Gen. Andrew Jackson, Florida's first Governor and later President of the United States. Call himself became a Territorial Governor and early leader of the state. He was a staunch Unionist, who opposed Florida's secession in 1861. He began construction of the home in 1825, which took some six years to finish. Call's daughter, Ellen Call Long, was born here, the first white child born in Tallahassee. She was known as "The Tallahassee Girl."

Williams was three weeks late. He caught up with Simmons, exploring on his own, at a Gadsden County plantation.

After inspecting the "old fields" in the Tallahassee area, spotting the lovely lakes, climbing the seven beautiful hills, finding a spring and cascade, they decided this was it. Especially convincing was the fact that Tallahassee is almost exactly midway between Saint Augustine and Pensacola.

In their report to the Council, the Commissioners wrote: "Tallahassee . . . a more beautiful country can scarcely be imagined; it is high, rolling, and well watered, the richness of the soil renders it so perfectly adapted to farming, that living must ultimately be cheap and abundant."

The report also noted: "Education will undoubtedly claim the early attention of the Legislature, and in no part of the world can it be fostered under happier auspices than on the gentle rolling hills and native lawns of Tallahassee."

There were about 500 Indians in the region at the time, and their leader was "a shrewd, penetrating man" called Chief Neamathla. An arrangement was worked out—and Tallahassee became the first and only capital of all Florida, so proclaimed by Governor DuVal on March 4, 1824.

[17]

The first white settlers, led by John McIver of North Carolina, arrived at the new town site on April 9, 1824, to be joined shortly thereafter by other pioneer planters.

Governor DuVal administered government from a boat at St. Marks until a log-cabin assembly hall was hastily erected for the 1824 Legislative Council, which convened on November 8, 1824.

Congress granted the new Territory a quarter section of land at the new capital site to be sold in order to raise money to provide the needed public buildings. The first sale took place in April 1825.

The official birthday of the municipality of Tallahassee would be December 9, 1825, the date it was incorporated, but it had been a going concern under federal officials for more than a year by that time.

The newcomers had hustled in putting together a fine village in those early months. By the time of its incorporation, Tallahassee proudly listed fifty houses, a church, a schoolhouse, two hotels, seven stores, an apothecary's shop, a printing office, two shoemakers, two blacksmiths, three carpenters, a tailor, and three brickyards. The State Capitol was the centerpiece of the humming community.

In the spring of that momentous year of 1825, the United States Congress granted to the Marquis de LaFayette a township of land in Tallahassee as a token of appreciation of his services in the Revolutionary War. The General planned to establish a free-labor colony of French peasants on the grant. He had hoped to prove his theory that free labor could be more productive than slave labor, then the mode of the times. LaFayette himself never came to Tallahassee. His project here failed and the property eventually was sold for $103,000. A county not too far from the capital city was named Lafayette in honor of the famed Frenchman; its county seat is Mayo.

It was soon recognized that the log cabin which housed the State government was inadequate, and plans were developed for a new Capitol. Col. Robert Butler, the Surveyor General of Florida, won a $100 prize for his design. A two-story wooden structure was erected in 1826, the Masonic lodge laying the cornerstone on January 7, 1826.

In its infancy, Tallahassee was a wild, rip-roaring frontier village. Malcolm Johnson, narrator of local history, noted that population was not long following the politicians. "It was the usual frontier comingling of rough adventurers and solid settlers," Johnson wrote, "but from all reports the ruffians exceeded the gentry and the little town's streets were the scene of duels, brawls, knife fights, and all the violence which came to characterize the wild and wooly west half a century later."

But the better citizens got the upper hand, partially because a yellow fever epidemic wiped out much of the roughneck element in 1841, but mostly because Thomas Jefferson's grandson, Francis Eppes, took over as the first reform mayor and cleaned up the place. They gave the chief executive the title

TALLAHASSEE street in 1838, drawn by Count de Castelnau. (LC)

FLORIDA'S SECOND CAPITOL building in 1838, in a drawing by Count de Castelnau. The plans were approved in 1825 for a building 40 x 26 feet, and the cornerstone was laid on January 7, 1826, with Masonic ceremonies. Although the sketch looks like that of a frame building, the old Capitol "was built with mortar made from lime burned in our immediate vicinity at the place known as the 'Cascades,' " according to a newspaper account in 1843. (LC)

of "intendent" at that time. A fire about this time also contributed to a change as it wiped out the shanty buildings north and east of the old Capitol.

Eppes was a Justice of Peace from 1833 to 1837 and it was during that time a grand jury presentment blistered the Marion Race Course. It was called "a public nuisance, a hotbed of vice, intemperance, gambling and profanity deserving the just censure of every lover of decency and good order."

Soon the word got around the Southland of the plantation opportunities of the fertile lands surrounding Tallahassee. This attracted people with the finest family names from the Carolinas, Virginia, and, not only from the South, but even New England. Patriots with illustrious names like Randolph, Byrd, Bradford, Winthrop, Henry, Whitfield, Branch, and Brevard—these and many more showed up.

One such glamorous personage was Prince Achille Murat, the nephew of Napoleon Bonaparte, who came here in 1825. The following year he married a young widow, Catharine Daingerfield Willis Gray, a great-grandniece of George Washington.

Prince Murat described Tallahassee living in those early days in a letter to friends in which he reported on elaborate parties and claimed the ladies were as beautiful and as well-dressed as any in New York. He also noted: "No news in town except a wine party, or rather, eating, drinking, card playing, and segar smoking."

A visitor here in 1827 was the famous writer Ralph Waldo Emerson. His impression of the city wasn't too favorable, though: "Tallahassee, a grotesque place, selected three years since as a suitable spot for the capital of the territory, and since that day rapidly settled by public officers, land speculators and desperados . . . Governor Duval is the button on which all things are hung."

Early efforts were made to meet transportation needs of the frontier community. The capital became the trade center of the area with St. Marks as the shipping point. Florida's first railroad, a mule-drawn affair, was built from Tallahassee to St. Marks. A plank road was later built between the two towns. The Federal Road came through the capital city as it wound its way from St. Augustine to Pensacola.

The primitive railroad got some "bad press" when the French artist, Count Castelnau, was a passenger in the spring of 1838. He labeled the railroad as "certainly the very worst that has been built in the entire world." But even he admired the builders for inspiring "a project of such a sort in a country inhabited by hostile savages and through almost impenetrable forests, which so few years ago were not even explored by the whites."

By 1839, Florida was ready to come into the Union as a State. It held a Constitutional Convention in St. Joseph and drafted its basic law. But she was coming in as a slave state and had to wait for a partner from the free side.

BELLEVUE THE OLD MURAT HOMESTEAD

REAL ROYALTY once graced Florida's capital. Prince Charles Louis Napoleon Achille Murat, a nephew of Napoleon Bonaparte, married Catherine Willis Gray, a grand-grand niece of George Washington, in Tallahassee in 1826. They built a country home in Jefferson county called "Lipona." The Princess bought "Bellevue" (*above*) in 1854, several years after Prince Murat's death in 1847. The beautiful mansion was built between 1838 and 1841.

CHARLES DOWNING was Florida's Territorial Delegate to Congress in 1839. It was Downing who obtained a $20,000 appropriation from Congress for the erection of a new Capitol.

TO THE PUBLIC.

The object of this placard is to inform the Public that Gen. Leigh Read has declined giving to me an apology for the insult offered me at St. Marks, on the 5th inst. That he has also refused to me that satisfaction, which as an honorable man, (refusing to apologise,) he was bound to give. I therefore pronounce him a Coward and a Scoundrel.

WILLIAM TRADEWELL.

Tallahassee, Oct. 26, 1839.

DUELING was a practice in the capital city in the Territorial days. Placards such as this one usually brought sparks. The Gen. Leigh Read mentioned here was involved in a famous duel with another political big-wig of the day, Col. Augustus Alston. Read was the victor in that contest, but lost his life to the son of his victim, Willis Alston, a short time later. A tough anti-dueling bill was introduced but failed to pass the next session of the Legislative Council.

LEON COUNTY was established as the seventh county in Florida on December 29, 1824, named in honor of Juan Ponce de Leon, discovered and namer of the state. The first Court House was occupied April 1833. It was built on the site of the present Post Office, on the north side of Park between Monroe and Adams. The old Court House burned in 1879.

It was not until 1845 that Iowa was ready to join the Union as a free state, and so Florida and Iowa came in that year, Florida being the 27th state.

The day we became a state, we were able to move into our sparkling new State Capitol which had been under construction since 1839. It is the oldest part of the Capitol and the center section of the building still being used today. (A new Capitol structure is presently under construction.)

William D. Moseley became Florida's first elected state Governor on June 25, 1845, and Tallahassee staged one of its most colorful inaugurals. A long parade featured such military units as the Quincy Lancers, the Tallahassee Guards, the Centreville Hussars, and the Leon Artillery. A feature of the parade was the marching of 28 school girls who represented the 26 states plus the new states of Florida and Iowa. The Grand Lodge of Masons was being held in the city at the time and participated in the celebration.

After Florida was admitted to the Union as a State, Tallahassee began to settle into a typical southern plantation-economy pattern. That was ended abruptly by the beginning of the Civil War, and secession along with the other Confederate states.

Florida's Capitol was the only Southern Capitol east of the Mississippi that was not captured by Federal troops during the Civil War. They tried, but were repelled in the Battle of Natural Bridge in March, 1865, when a Federal expedition marched against the city from the St. Mark's River.

A "pick-up army" composed of citizens, cadets from the West Florida Seminary (now Florida State University), and a few regular troops turned back the Federals. The Stars and Bars of the Confederacy continued to wave over the Capitol for only two months until May 20, 1865, when Federal military authorities occupied the town after the close of hostilities.

After the war, Reconstruction and Carpetbag rule came to Florida and its little capital, but not as harshly as it was administered in older Southern states.

The hotly-disputed election of 1876 was the breaking point of the grip of the Carpetbaggers in Florida. In this historic event, the upshot was that the nation got a Republican President—Rutherford B. Hayes—while Florida got a Democratic Governor—George F. Drew. There were charges of election frauds in many parts of the state and the undertone that in the final analysis, Florida made a "deal" with the powers-that-be at the national level for the swap-out that brought Florida state government back under the Democrats. The closeness of the national contest put the spotlight on Florida and on Tallahassee during the counting and recounting of the returns and the legal battles that followed. Politicians of national stature and famed political reporters jammed Tallahassee. The busy City Hotel hired 45 waiters to serve the influx.

In 1875, a well-known Southern poet and writer, Sidney Lanier, arrived.

He was putting together a tourist guide of the state. He was impressed with Tallahassee—especially with its hospitality.

"The repute of these (Tallahassee) people for hospitality was a matter of national renown before the war between the States; and even the dreadful reverses of that cataclysm appear to have spent their force in vain against this feature of Tallahassee manners; for much testimony since the war—to which this writer cheerfully adds his own—goes to show that it exists unimpaired.

"Genuine hospitality of this sort is indeed as unconquerable as Zeno's problem of Achilles and the Tortoise is unanswerable. The logic of it is that if there is enough for ten, there is certainly enough for eleven; and if enough for eleven, enough for twelve; and so on *ad infinitum*; and this reasoning has such a mysterious virtue in it, that it has compassed among good-hearted folk many a repetition of the miracle of the loaves and fishes."

And Sidney Lanier continued: "It really appears to have been a serious question here, just after the war had completely upset the whole productive system and stunned every energy of the land, of what avail would so little be among so many; but no one has starved, and albeit the people are poor and the dwellings need paint and ready money is slow of circulation, yet it must be confessed that the bountiful tables looked like anything but famine, that signs of energy cropped out here and there in many places, and that the whole situation was but a reasonable one for a people who ten years ago had to begin life anew from the very bottom, with no capital, and with a set of laborers who had gone into politics to such an extent that their field-duties were often interrupted by taking their seats in the Legislature, or by other cares of office incompatible with the plow and the hoe."

We get another glimpse of Tallahassee during this period from another writer, a newspaper reporter named George M. Barbour, who produced the interesting volume *Florida for Tourists, Invalids and Settlers*. He instantly tabbed Tallahassee as "the floral city of the flowery South" and proclaimed it one of the loveliest places in all America.

A brief excerpt from Barbour's description of the capital city reads: "It is an unpretentious old city, with an air of village-like rustic simplicity; no factories (except one cotton-mill); all is quiet, country life. The residence avenues are mostly lined with cozy little cottages, and comfortable, roomy, substantial mansions of the good old-time style of architecture, and all are surrounded by neatly fenced lawns and gardens, almost all having quite ample grounds, well kept—and flowers, flowers, flowers!"

Reporter Barbour also took note of the lovely suburbs and then commented on the countryside which he saw as "a vast range of hills, valleys, brooks, lakes, park-like clusters of large trees, broad, well-cultivated fields, large plantation dwellings and cotton-gins, and distant forests—in all, a remarkably beautiful natural panorama of nature, such as is seen nowhere else in Florida."

CONSTRUCTION OF THE PRESENT CAPITOL was begun in 1839, six years before Florida was admitted to the Union as a State. Note there was no dome on the original building. This is the center section of the historic Capitol.

FLORIDA STATE UNIVERSITY had its beginning on January 24, 1851, when the Legislature passed a law establishing two seminaries, one east and one west of the Suwannee River. A fight developed over the location, Marianna and Quincy vying with Tallahassee and it wasn't until 1857 that the doors of West Florida Seminary opened. Here is the first building. It stood about where Westcott Building now stands and was turned over to the Seminary by the City. The building's brick walls became badly cracked because of a faulty foundation. It was replaced in 1891 by a red brick building, College Hall, and eventually by Westcott. Originally the Seminary was for males only but after charges of sex discrimination it opened a separate female department. Subsequently it was known as Literary College of Florida University, Florida State College and Florida Female College. In 1909 it became Florida State College for Women which lasted until 1947 when it once again became coeducational and assumed its present name.

A HANDSOME CADET at West Florida Seminary. The young students were heroes at the Battle of Natural Bridge near the end of the Civil War. They were credited with being responsible for saving the Capitol of Florida from capture by Northern forces.

CAPT. PATRICK HOUSTON was one of the leaders of the Confederates in the fierce Battle of Natural Bridge. A Tallahassee resident, he was a lineal descendent of Sir Patrick Houston, and was a kinsman to John Houston McIntosh of Fort George Island. (Dunn)

CONFEDERATE COMMANDER at the Battle of Natural Bridge was Gen. William Miller. He had about 500 men, and three of them were reported killed. (Dunn)

The visiting journalist bragged about the unique floral fair held in the city each spring. He topped off his evaluation of Tallahassee with the conclusion: "Nowhere is there a more refined and cultured society than in Tallahassee."

Periodically throughout its history, Tallahassee has had to fight off attempts to remove the State Capitol. An effort was made at the very first session held in the new capital city, in 1824, "to remove the seat of government to a site on some navigable water."

The latest attempt came in 1967 when a State Senator from Miami, Lee Weissenborn, moaned that "Tallahassee makes you sleepy." He added that "the thinking here is to the right of Louis XIV." But his attempt to remove the capital failed as many others have.

Serious efforts were made in 1843 and 1881, but the movement in 1900 actually brought about a referendum. Tallahassee received a clear majority partly because the other cities vying for the honor ripped each other to shreds in the hot campaign. The vote was Tallahassee, 16,742; Jacksonville, 7,675; Ocala, 4,917, and St. Augustine, 2,881.

Someone noted that seldom has a site for a city been deliberately selected, less often has it been chosen in a wilderness, and scarcely ever has a capital been placed not only many miles from any settlement but far from any single habitation of civilized men. Yet thus it was with Tallahassee when its site was chosen for the seat of government of the Territory of Florida and as the permanent home of its wandering Council.

It is conceded here that Tallahassee is probably the most isolated of the 50 capitals in its proximity to heavily-populated areas. It lies 170 miles from Jacksonville, 200 from Pensacola, 240 from Tampa, 245 from Orlando, 460 from Miami and 606 miles from Key West. It lies only 20 miles from the Georgia line.

In her book, *The Other Florida*, Gloria Jahoda refers to the capital city being "two hundred miles from anywhere else."

In 1915, there was agitation to split Florida into two states. The venerable editor of *The Tampa Daily Times*, D. B. McKay, editorialized at the time that Tampa would make a good site for the capital of "South Florida" and he suggested that the old Tampa Bay Hotel (now University of Tampa) be conveyed to the new State. Nothing came of the idea.

Even as these periodic efforts to remove the capital took place, Tallahassee moved to nail down forevermore its prize with the continuing development of a Capitol Center. Concludes Malcolm Johnson: "The new Constitution and development of the Capitol Center now underway—along with realization of easier transportation from all points—seems to have fixed the city on the map forever as Capital of Florida." So be it.

In the past century, growth and development of Tallahassee has been more steady than spectacular—as measured by the boom economy of other parts of Florida.

ST. JOHN'S Episcopal Church was incorporated in 1829, and a new building was opened with divine services on May 7, 1838. The church was of wood "in the Grecian order, with a portico with four pillars." It was destroyed by fire in 1879. (Johnson)

Johnson noted that even while the rest of Florida was booming in the 1920s, Tallahassee was a sleepy little town of slow, gracious living tailored to accommodation of a genteel Florida State College for Women student body and a surge of political and social activity every other year when the Legislature came into session.

The town took off in a flurry of growth after World War II when FSCW was converted into the co-educational FSU that now has attained a national reputation for some graduate fields of study, and top ranking in intercollegiate sports.

Facing page: TALLAHASSEE in the 1870s as it looked from the steps of the State Capitol.

[28]

Tallahassee before 1900

THE CITY HOTEL was one of the most popular hostelries. Built about 1828 as Pindar's Florida Hotel, it was bought by Thomas Brown, a future Governor (1849-53). He expanded it and named it Brown's Inn, or City Hotel. Located at Pensacola and Adams, across the street from the Capitol, it was later known as the Morgan Hotel, and even later as the Adelphi. It burned down in 1886. Among its famous guests were the Count de Castelnau who, in the winter of 1837-38, called it the best tavern in town. Alabama poet Sidney Lanier described it as "a genuine old-fashioned tavern," with an air of ease and comfort. Political pots boiled for half a century in this hotel. During the Hayes-Tilden election contest in 1876, when Florida's vote was crucial, politicians and reporters from all over the country converged upon Tallahassee in such numbers that the hotel had to employ 45 waiters to serve them.

A LOT OF ACTION took place at Washington Square where commuters "parked" their horses and vehicles for a day of shopping and visiting in the city.

THE RANDALL HOUSE at 424 N. Calhoun Street boasted the first inside bathroom in Tallahassee. The house was built for Thomas Randall, a Federal Judge of the Territory of Florida. It was begun about 1837 and completed before 1840. The Randall House earned the distinction of having the first indoor plumbing perhaps in all Florida, with water furnished from a windmill in the backyard, when it was owned by George Lewis, a prominent banker here. This photo of the house was taken in 1870.

THE CAPITOL GROUNDS were heavily shaded by large trees in 1870. Someone has noted that the Capitol stood for 56 years as a plain, three-story building "hardly distinguished from any affluent county's courthouse." Six doric columns graced the front and rear entrances.

HARRIET BEECHER STOWE, the author of Uncle Tom's Cabin, got a big welcome on the steps of the Florida State Capitol in 1874. President Abraham Lincoln called her "the little lady who started a big war," and her name was anathema in Florida before the Civil War. But in 1867 she was wintering in Florida and had an estate on the St. Johns River at Mandarin. She is seen here, the lady in black on the sixth step, being greeted by Gov. Marcellus L. Stearns, center front on steps, a Republican. Mrs. Stowe's brother, the Rev. Charles Beecher, served as State Superintendent of Public Instruction in 1871-72.

THE CHURCH OF SAINT MARY, shown in this 1870 photo, stood at the northeast corner of Park Avenue and Gadsden Street. It was built in 1854 by Capt. R. A. Shine. The Catholics had a small church as early as 1846, named in honor of the Sorrowful Mother. It burned down in 1847 and the local paper, the *Sentinel,* lamented: "The church just destroyed was a more than ordinary achievement of the handful of Catholics in Tallahassee. They are few and generally poor."

THE MARKET PLACE in what is now Bloxham Park was the hub of activity in the early days of Tallahassee. This is a view showing the market place and the First Presbyterian Church.

MARKET PLACE
TALLAHASSEE

"THE COLUMNS" was the handsome home of William "Money" Williams, a pioneer Tallahassee banker. The mansion, of Greek revival architecture, was built in 1835 by contractor Benjamin Chaires from North Carolina. It stood at 105 West Park Avenue at Adams, but was moved to Duval and Park in the early 1970s when it was acquired by the Tallahassee Chamber of Commerce for its headquarters. Tradition has it that a nickel is imbedded in every brick, arising probably from the remark made by the contractor that every brick was worth a nickel.

THE "BOWEN HOUSE" at 325 N. Calhoun Street was occupied at one time by Capt. Charles Edward Dyke, the editor of *The Floridian* and one of the state's great journalists. Built by James Kirksey in the early 1830s with white pine lumber from Maine, it was pre-fabricated in New York City, and believed to be the oldest pre-fab structure in the state. Captain Dyke sold it in 1885 to Newton Marion Bowen, an old-time employee of *The Floridian* regarded as "the most ethical editor south of Baltimore." Photo shows Mrs. Bowen (right) and daughter, Miss Nettie Claire Bowen. (Johnson)

UNTIL 1907, Florida did not provide an executive mansion for its governors, so they made their own arrangements for accommodations. Today, it is believed only one of these homes remains where governors stayed during their administrations. It is the building at 410 Calhoun Street, where Gov. William D. Bloxham lived through two terms (1881-85) and (1897-1901). Bloxham bought the house some fifty years after it was built in the late 1830s by David C. Wilson, founder of Florida's oldest department store. It is also believed that Gov. E. A. Perry (1885-89) occupied the house.

AN ELABORATE FLOAT for an early parade was this one by J. D. Cay, a wholesale and retail dealer in buggies, harness and saddles. (Johnson)

THEY LIKED TO SHOW OFF their oxen in the olden days. This group of Tallahassee "dudes" makes an interesting group posing in front of a beautiful mansion. (Johnson)

THE CREW OF ENGINE NO. 16 of the Florida Railway and Navigation Company of Tallahassee pauses for picture-taking in 1886. Two little lads join in the occasion.

THE MARKET, now Bloxham Park, was the congregating point downtown in the late 1880s. That is a corner of the handsome Leon Hotel showing at the left.

OFFICERS of a black lodge pose for a formal portrait. The banner announced it as "Hannah's Court, APA." (Johnson)

OLD TIMERS SAY this building is perhaps the Bethel A.M.E. Church (Negro) which stood at the corner of Virginia and Duval. The pastor and the congregation are being photographed along with the handsome building. (Johnson)

ALL DRESSED UP and ready to go to town before the turn of the century. (Johnson)

A TALLAHASSEE MATRON in the early days wears flowers on her dress and a bejeweled comb in her hair as she has her portrait made. (Johnson)

A HANDSOME FAMILY all decked out in their finery. (Johnson)

RAPID TRANSIT, no less, was this oxen and wagon shown in front of the southeast corner of Adams and College. One of the men has been identified as a Tully, the father of Emerson G. and Leon C. Tully. (Johnson)

BUSY MONROE STREET pauses from a business day as merchants and shoppers stand rigidly to have their picture snapped. This is between Park and College. (Johnson)

AT ONE TIME Tallahassee had a cigar factory, owned by A. Wahnish. (Johnson)

STREET SCENE IN THE 1880s, showing the East side of Monroe between Park Avenue (then known as McCarthy) and Call. Kemper's Stable and Saint John's Episcopal Church are easily seen. Note the street car rumbling down the main drag. (Johnson)

THE FIRST COURT HOUSE burned in 1879 and the old Leon Hotel was built on the site. The building shown here is the first court house built on the present Leon County Court House site, erected in 1883. This is the scene from the dome of the State Capitol.

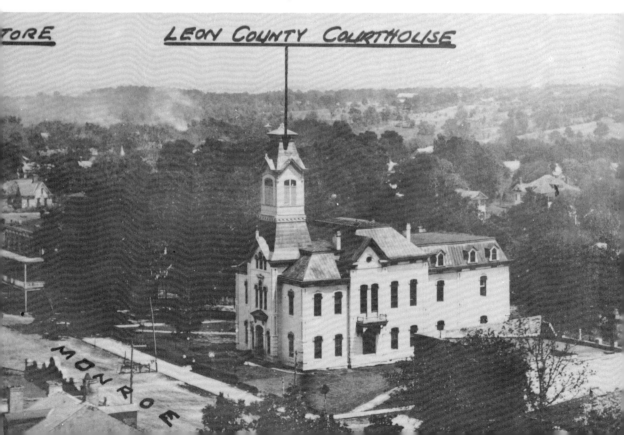

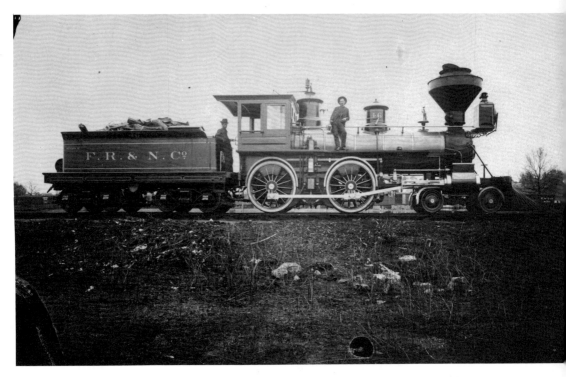

THE FLORIDA RAILWAY AND NAVIGATION COMPANY had up-to-date equipment and proudly showed it off for photographer Harper in the late 1880s. Engine No. 46 is pictured with its proud crew, while Engine No. 28, pulling a passenger car, is shown with both the crew and passengers posing.

HORSE-DRAWN STREET CAR provided mass transit for the capital city in the 1880s.

CYCLISTS before the turn of the century: Captain Strum and Laurie Perkins with an unidentified friend.

[44]

ALLIGATOR POINT on the Gulf of Mexico has long been a recreation spot for Tallahassee. (Johnson)

"POSTURING IN THE PARK" is the title of this A. S. Harper photo of the 1880s. This photograph was one of several made here that was selected by Time-Life for a volume, "This Fabulous Century 1870-1900." The park picture is thought to have been made in Slusser's Pasture, adjacent to present Franklin Boulevard. Gov. and Mrs. Edward A. Perry who served 1885-89 are believed to be among the hatted and bustled women and derby-wearing men shown gathered on and around a fallen tree.

PICNICKING IN THE PARK was a pleasant pastime in Tallahassee in 1888. Here are shown wagons arriving for a day at Llewellyn Park.

FOR INAUGURATION of Gov. E. A. Perry, a Confederate hero, on Jan. 6, 1885, these pretty Tallahassee lassies paraded with American flag made of silk worms grown in the capital city. The first two girls have been identified as Jane Brevard Darby and Alice Brevard Gwynn.

[47]

BEARDS AND MOUSTACHES were in vogue in 1887 when members of the Legislature posed for this photograph.

THE 1889 STATE SENATE—but who's the nice-looking lady in the first row at right?

A FINE FARM in Leon County back in the late 1800s is shown in this A. W. Harper photograph.

DOWNTOWN TALLAHASSEE in March 1888—Monroe Street at College (than called Clinton Avenue). Landmarks include the First Presbyterian Church and the ornate Leon Hotel on the site of the present Post Office.

"LOOK PRETTY, GIRLS," admonishes the photographer, and this pair of Tallahassee lassies respond beautifully. (Johnson)

THE FAIN HOUSE at the northeast corner of College and Calhoun is still standing. It forms the backdrop for a pleasing family portrait. (Johnson)

A HAPPY FAMILY GROUP is posing among the flowers in an early Tallahassee setting. (Johnson)

AN ATTRACTIVE TALLAHASSEE
socialite was Miss Laura Barnes who was
to become Mrs. Arvah Hopkins. This formal portrait was taken in January, 1889.

THE YOUNGER GENERATION—
note the high-wheeled baby carriage,
along with a matching doll carriage.
(Johnson)

OLD-TIME DIGNITARIES: Among those identified is H. Clay Crawford, for many years the Secretary
of State. He is the gentleman with the moustache on the lower step. Park Trammell, on the top step, was
Attorney General, Governor, and U.S. Senator. He also was Mayor of Lakeland, a member of the House
of Representatives, and President of the 1905 State Senate. This photo may have been made about the turn
of the century. (Johnson)

"THE GREAT DEMOCRATIC NEWSPAPER OF FLORIDA" was an apt slogan for *The Weekly Floridian*, which in the 1880s was printed in this neat building at the northwest corner of Monroe and Pensacola. *The Floridian* had been established in 1828, and a year later was merged with the *Florida Advocate*, which really was the pioneer *Florida Intelligencer* under a new name. For three-quarters of a century *The Floridian* was Florida's most influential paper, according to Malcom B. Johnson, editor of present-day *Tallahassee Democrat. The Floridian's* name lives today, by virtue of continuous publication and clear transfer of title, on the masthead of the *St. Petersburg Times* Sunday magazine. *The Floridian* was Democrat, and stayed loyal to the Southern viewpoint through the war under the ownership of Charles E. Dyke, who has been called "Nestor of the Florida Press" and "walking encyclopedia of Florida," because of his first-hand acquaintance with the state's history and politics. Dyke was the first president of the Florida Press Association, which was organized in 1880. He sold the *Floridian* in 1883 to Newton M. Bowen and died four years later. Bowen was president of the FPA in 1889.

E. H. ALFORD'S department store is one of the oldest businesses in Tallahassee. It was located on the West side of Monroe Street between Jefferson and College Streets. Presumably, the gents in this photo taken before the turn of the century are the clerks of the store.

MONROE STREET in the 1880s, on the west side between Pensacola and Jefferson. Firms shown include the Floridian Printing Co., J. Burkhardt Merchant Tailor, Fashionable Dressmaking (upstairs) and Bargain Store, Dry Goods, and Groceries. The City water tank is shown on roof.

POPULAR WATERING HOLE in the 1880s was The Leon Liquor Store, Bar and Pool Room on the southwest corner of Monroe at College. It later became Bennett's Corner. (Johnson)

MOTHER AND BABY greet dad as he arrives by horseback at a Tallahassee home in the 1880s. Shady trees made the area attractive and peaceful.

THE LEON HOTEL.

1 Capitol.
2 County Court House.
3 University of Florida.
4 State Seminary.
5 Lincoln Academy.
6 University Library.
7 Gallie's Hall.
8 Masonic and I. O. O. F. Hall.
9 Post Office.
10 Depot F. R. & N. Co. and St. Marks R. R.
11 Leon Hotel.   J. M. Lee, Prop.
12 "The Morgan." Geo. C. Morgan, Prop.

13 St. James Hotel.   George A. Lamb, Prop.
14 Episcopal Church.
15 Presbyterian Church.
16 Methodist Church.
17 Baptist Church.
18 Catholic Church and Convent.
19 Colored Methodist Churches.
20 Colored Baptist Churches.
21 "The Murat Place,"—"Residence of Prince Murat, son
   of the king of Naples.
22 Graves of Prince and Princess Murat.
23 Site of Fort San Luis.
9 The Floridian Office.
24 The Land of Flowers Office.

COPYRIGHTED & PUBLISHED BY NORRIS, WI

VIEW OF

TALLAH

STATE CAPIT

COUNTY SE

300 Feet A

BECK & PAULI

L.Nº 107 WELLS ST.MILWAUKEE,WIS,1885.

ITY OF

ASSEE.

FLORIDA.

EON COUNTY.

.

Sea Level.

ilwaukee.Wis.

THE MORGAN.

25 The Economist Office.
26 B. C. Lewis and Sons, Bankers.
27 The Tallahassee Real Estate Exchange.
28 Wm. P. Slusser & Co., General Merchandise.
29 M. Lively, Drugs and Medicines.
30 R. & J. Munro, General Merchandise.
31 Cole S.Dickenson, General Merchandise.
32 Y. A. Levy, General Merchandise.
33 A. Gallie Jr., General Merchandise and Bakery.
34 Geo. P. Raney, Judge Supreme Court.
35 D. S. Walker, Judge Circuit Court.
36 C. A. Bryan, Clerk of Circuit Court.

37 R. W. Williams, Attorney at Law.
27 John A. Henderson, Attorney at Law.
39 F.T. Myers, Attorney at Law.
40 Geo. W. Betton, M. D.
41 T. J. Perkins, Commission Merchant.
42 J. C. Kemper, Livery Stable.
43 Geo. Lewis' Residence.
44 Edward Lewis' Residence.
45 W. C. Lewis' Residence.
46 R. C. Long's Residence.
47 R. W. Williams' Residence.
48 D. Cook's Residence.
49 F. R. & N. R. R. Shops.

THE RESIDENTIAL SECTION of Tallahassee in the 1880s (*above*). Note the street car tracks in both pictures—the capital city was served by mass transit then. *Below*: Another view, possibly Monroe Street. A canopy of oaks provided shade for the peaceful neighborhood.

A TENANT FARM HOUSE in the countryside around Tallahassee in the 1880s.

HORSE AND BUGGY DAYS in the capital offered such scenes as this in the residential section. Picket fences were popular.

"A SUPERB SURVIVAL" of the mid-nineteenth century is the handsome McDougall House at 329 N. Meridian Street. Since it was built in 1850, it was in the same family until the early 1970s when the State of Florida bought it for the Historic Tallahassee Preservation Board, which has executive offices there. The original owner was Peres B. Brokaw. Lumber, the massive Corinthian pillars, doors, cornices, and bronze chandeliers were all imported from London. Architectural features include the hip roof and captain's walk, the crocker cornices with pendants, the pediments over the windows (an echo of Greek Revival influence), front windows extending to the floor, and the one-story porch running across the front with fluted Corinthian columns. (Dunn)

"GOODWOOD" on East Miccosukee Road is one of Tallahassee's most beautiful plantation homes. Hardy Bryan Croom, a distinguished botanist, built the mansion for his family on land that was once a part of the Lafayette Grant. Construction was halted by Croom's death at sea in 1837, in the tragic sinking of the steamship *Home*. It was finally completed about 1843 by his brother, Bryan. Note the "widow's walk" on the roof.

STUDENTS at West Florida Seminary: The Naturalists Club of 1897.

COLLEGE HALL in the 1890s was the only building of the West Florida Seminary, which became Florida State College in 1901, Florida Female College in 1905, and finally Florida State University. College Hall was replaced by Wescott Hall in 1909. (Johnson)

[61]

THEY BROKE GROUND for a new Post Office at 10:30 a.m. on April 16, 1892. The building was at the southeast corner of Adams and Park. Some of those present are Mayor R. B. Carpenter (1); City Marshall Henry Burneuter (2); Constantine Algero, proprietor of the Constantine House (6); and Thomas Costa, proprietor of Costa's restaurant (9). (Johnson)

THE FOUNDATION IS POURED for the Post Office. The mansion in the background at left is "The Columns," and the church is the First Presbyterian. (Johnson)

THE POST OFFICE in 1898. It served later as the Tallahassee City Hall and finally was demolished in 1964.

J. C. KEMPER'S Livery Stable in 1898, with St. John's Episcopal Church in the background. It's on the east side of Monroe between Call and Park. Monroe Street was not paved until 1912 or 1913 and then only after much civic controversy and a referendum vote. The street was leveled, a cushion of sand put down, and then bricks were laid closely and rolled into the clay and sand.

"Babes in the wood"

THEY WERE NOT 'BABES IN THE WOOD' as indicated in this caption penciled by some unknown in the past. These were members of the 1891 Florida State Senate who played hookey to avoid a confrontation vote in the hot U.S. Senatorial election of that year. In those days, there was a feud between some members of the State Legislature and the incumbent U.S. Sen. Wilkinson Call, descendant of former Gov. Richard Keith Call. The politicians shown in this photo are said to be the members who, by going to Georgia, sought to evade the Sergeant-at-arms, thus preventing a quorum and blocking the election of Call. Call eventually was declared the winner after other shenanigans had taken place.

[64]

PRESIDENT WILLIAM McKINLEY visited Tallahassee on March 24, 1899, and posed with friends on the steps of the Florida State Capitol. Those identified in the photo include 1., J. R. Cohen; 2., Gen. Richard Scarlitt; 3., Guyte McLendon; 4., Mrs. Mark Hanna; 5., Sen. Mark Hanna; 6., Mrs. McKinley; 7., Mrs. W. D. Bloxham; 8., President McKinley; 9., Secretary George B. Cortelyou; 10., Gov. W. D. Bloxham; 11., E. M. Hopkins, and 12., W. R. Wilson.

SOME WAG called this "The most attractive feature of the President's visit" the day President William McKinley visited Tallahassee on March 24, 1899. The patriotic black man is unidentified.

ICE AND SNOW IN FLORIDA! Yes, it did snow on February 13, 1899. First the dignified gentlemen from the State Capitol posed for a picture on the State House steps, and then, suddenly, an old-fashioned snowball fight broke out! And the fountain on the Capitol grounds froze over solid—a rare sight indeed.

Jefferson Street and Court House, Tallahassee, Fla.

TALLAHASSEE AT TURN OF THE CENTURY. This is looking down Jefferson Street towards the Leon County Court House, from Adams Street. The famed Monroe Opera House is on the left, while on the right is the City Market and Fire Station. (Johnson)

THE OLD LEON COUNTY COURT HOUSE was a handsome structure. (Johnson)

TALLAHASSEE was a hamlet of 3000 inhabitants in 1900. These panoramic views show (*top*) Main Street with the Leon County Court House, the Bloxham Hotel in the center, and the "Southern Express Company" in the building at right. *Center*: The State Capitol and grounds surrounding it. *Bottom*: The First Presbyterian church at left, the old Leon Hotel at center, and the old Post Office (later City Hall) at right. (Johnson)

[68]

Tallahassee from 1900-1920

ANOTHER SPLENDID HOSTELRY serving the community at the turn of the century was the magnificent St. James Hotel (*above*) at the northeast corner of Monroe and Jefferson. This photo shows it in 1898. It was later named the Bloxham Hotel in honor of the Tallahassean who served two terms as Governor of Florida from 1881 to 85 and from 1897 to 1901. The Bloxham Hotel (*below*) attracted many prominent politicians and others during its heyday. It also was known as a commercial hotel with a clientele largely made up of "drummers" or traveling men. It set a good table, guests reported. At one time it was managed by George A. and Fanny W. Lamb. A street car track ran by the hotel.

FOR SEVERAL DECADES, the impressive Leon Hotel was a popular hostelry in Tallahassee. It was built on the site where the Post Office is now after the first County Court House burned there in 1879. The Leon also burned, in 1925. An article printed in 1911 noted of the Leon: "During the course of its life as a public hostelry all the distinguished men in Florida's public life and not a few personages of national renown have been its guests. The undercurrents of affairs at the Florida capital have eddied and swirled about the Leon; its lobbies have been the arena of famous gatherings and exciting occurrences; its walls have witnessed the making of slates that have built and broken political fortunes. It is full of romance and memories. Its vine covered galleries have offered delightful seclusion for many trysts, and its ball rooms have gathered through a long period of years the maidens and gallants of each succeeding generation for the healthful exhilaration of the dance." The clerk shown in the photo (*above*) is identified as a Mr. Oglesby. Automobiles had become frequent in the early 1900s, when the photo (*below*) was taken. It also shows the City Band Stand where prominent politicians held forth.

[71]

A 1901 PARADE down muddy Monroe Street was probably for the inauguration of Gov. William S. Jennings. This is looking north down Monroe. The Leon Guards are in formation in front of the County Court House at right of photo.

THE STATE CAPITOL received a cupola in 1891 (above) which was replaced by a dome in 1901-1902, at which time the north and south wings were also built.

THE OLD ST. AUGUSTINE ROAD is typical of many country roads over the hills and valleys around Tallahassee.

THE CIRCUS IS COMING! Gaily colored circus wagons are parading down Monroe Street in front of the old Leon Hotel in 1901.

A PEACEFUL SCENE on East Park Avenue in Tallahassee in the early 1900s.

On East Park Avenue, Tallahassee, Fla.

A FINE OLD RESORT hotel at Panacea Spring attracted Tallahasseans around the turn of the century. The distinguished gentleman in the front seat of the wagon may have been Gen. John P. S. Houston, Adjutant General of Florida. (Johnson)

THE "BATHING POOL," a delightful spot at Panacea Spring. (Johnson)

THE FLORIDA AGRICULTURAL AND MECHANICAL UNIVERSITY—nicknamed "FAMU"—was chartered as Florida State Normal and Industrial School for Negro Youth in 1887. In 1891 it moved to its present site, formerly the plantation of Territorial Gov. William P. Duval. Here is a photo of Gibb's Hall (*above*) of Florida Normal and Industrial School, and an early view (below). The school was placed under the management of the State Board of Control (now Regents) in 1905 as a co-educational college and then offered its first college-level instruction. (Johnson—FSU Library)

TALLAHASSEE BASEBALL TEAM of
the early days. Among those identified are
O. M. Jacobie, Guyte McCord, Ralph
Gramling, E. B. Cascer, Hugh Wilson,
Walter McLin, Peres McDougall, and
Howard Sheets.

THE "SEMINOLES" OF OLD? State college football in Tallahassee dates back many decades. Here is
the determined football squad of 1903 at Florida State College.

THE LAST CO-ED CLASS of Florida State College was the one of 1905 (*above*) which was also the first to wear caps and gowns for graduation. After graduation, FSC became Florida State College for Women until 1947 when it was converted into the co-educational Florida State University. Classes of this institution are still being held on the original campus where the Institute West of the Suwannee opened in 1857. Left to right in the picture are (seated): Miss N. Clare Bowen, Robert B. McCord, Miss Grace Cramer, Frank Gammon, Mrs. Agnes Apthorp Proctor, and (standing) Miss Ruby Diamond, Burton Belcher, Arthur (Joe) Shutan, David Cook, William Byrd, and Mrs. Bershe Meginniss Oven. The Class of 1905 met again 60 years later, at the homecoming banquet (*left*), and shown are from left to right: Mrs. W. J. Owen of Tallahassee; Robert B. McCord of Hapeville, Georgia; Miss N. Clare Bowen and Miss Ruby Diamond, both of Tallahassee.

FLORIDA STATE COLLEGE students studying hard in the library sometime during the period, 1901-05.

TALLAHASSEE ORGANIZED a volunteer fire department in 1902. The first fire house was a two-story frame shed located where the State-owned Martin Building now stands. This photo shows, left to right, Ernest McClain, C. A. Spencer, the first fire chief, an engineer who came here to supervise installation of a City water system and stayed to serve as the first fire chief, as well as water and gas superintendent; Lewis Lively and hose wagon driver Eugene Levy.

GALLANT FIREEATERS of 1906 pose for photo. Those who have been identified include Fred Levy, George Lewis, Ernest McClain, W. A. Bass, Alex S. Ferrell, Bill Phillips, D. M. Lowry, Fred Hardee, L. M. Lively, John C. Moor, Eugene Levy, Willie McIntosh, A. C. Spiller, J. G. Hamlin, Dr. F. C. Moor, and Paul Nicholson.

THE FIRST TWO-HORSE FIRE WAGON is seen here in 1905 in front of the old Leon County Court House. The horses were "Tom" and "Jerry." Aboard are Eugene Levy, Assistant Chief W. P. Phillips, Chief John Hamlin, the sanitary department superintendent who succeeded Spencer as fire chief about this time, an unidentified fireman, and Willie McIntosh.

MOTORIZATION OF THE FIRE DEPARTMENT began about 1915. This unidentified photo appears to be the fire chief racing to the scene of a fire in a horseless carriage.

A FUTURE GOVERNOR was among members of the 1903 House of Representatives posing for this picture, along with their attaches. Albert W. Gilchrist, third from right on front row holding hat with both hands, was Speaker of the 1903 House, and went on to become Governor (1909-13). He was from Punta Gorda.

[83]

NAPOLEON BONAPARTE BROWARD, one of Florida's most colorful and most controversial governors, was inaugurated on January 3, 1905. Broward (right) takes oath from Justice J. B. Whitfield. Partly obscured by Broward's elbow, at right, is Secretary of State H. Clay Crawford. To the right of Crawford, full-face in front of column is retiring Gov. William S. Jennings.

GOVERNOR BROWARD and family on the Mansion steps (*left*). During his administration, the State erected its first Executive Mansion on Adams Street. Started in 1906, it was not ready for occupancy until September, 1907. Meanwhile, Elizabeth Hutchinson Broward, sitting on her mother's lap, was the first child born to an incumbent Governor. She was born August 31, 1906, eighth of nine children of the Governor, at the family's residence on Monroe Street. The Mansion was designed by Jacksonville architect H. J. Klutho at a cost of $21,000. The construction crew (*below*) pauses for a pose.

A TRAVELER visiting the capital in April, 1907, sent this post card (*above*) of Saint John's Episcopal Church to a friend in Orlando and scribbled on top: "Looks old, but—so does the whole town!" The same visitor sent this post card (*below*) of the State Capitol with a caption reading: "Nice view of the 'joint.'" (Dunn)

THE TALLAHASSEE COUNTRY CLUB was organized as a private club in 1907. The third tee was one of the nine-hole golf course. It is now the 15th of the 18-hole Capital City Country Club course.

LEWIS PARK in Tallahassee was a nice spot for a stroll in 1909.

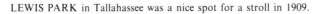

Real Cold here
this morning

"REAL COLD HERE THIS MORNING" was the notation on a post card showing Monroe Street in 1910. A few automobiles had made the scene by then, but Monroe was not to be paved until a couple years later. Monroe, by the way, was named for President Monroe who was in office when Florida was acquired in 1821.

A FLURRY OF ACTIVITY around the Seaboard Air Line Railway depot always took place when the passenger train arrived, as here in 1910.

S.A.L. Depot. Tallahassee, Fla.

FLORIDA STATE COLLEGE FOR
WOMEN in 1906: Girls and faculty con-
gregate on the steps of East Hall (*left*);
East Hall in 1912 (*center*). This building
went up in flames one Sunday morning
during church hour in 1919. Bryan Hall
(*bottom*) was constructed in 1907.

THE MAIN GATE at Florida State
College for Women after 1911. Wescott
Hall is in the background.

TENNIS, ANYONE? It was a determined
group of young coeds who formed the
Tennis Club at Florida State College for
Women in the year 1912.

Opening of
Millinery and Fancy Goods
Wednesday, October 12
Miss Adele Gerard
149 N. Monroe Street, Tallahassee, Fla.

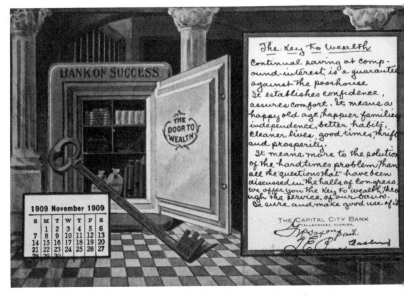

COME, GIRLS, A NEW STORE is opening in town. The announcement of October 1910 was in the form of a post card (*left*) and told of Miss Adele Gerard's new Millinery and Fancy Goods Shop at 149 N. Monroe Street, while this 1909 advertisement (*right*) by The Capital City Bank promises that "Continental saving at compound interest is a guarantee against the poorhouse."

LEON COUNTY EXHIBIT at the Marianna Fair in 1915 was put together by Mrs. Will Roberts, first full-time Home Demonstration Agent for Leon County. Her prize-winning exhibit included 53 varieties of canned products of Leon soil, fruit juices, and catsups.

"THE COLUMNS" at 105 West Park Avenue, in the early 1900s.

THE PRIDE OF TALLAHASSEE was the fine Cherokee Hotel on the south side of Park Avenue between Monroe and Calhoun. Legislators, famous personages, and numerous others stayed here during its heyday. The old hostelry was torn down in the 1950s.

ANOTHER OUTSTANDING HOTEL, this one still serving the public, is the Floridan on Monroe Street. Politics and other news of the day get an airing as guests from all over the state sit in rocking chairs on the long verandah and discuss events of the day.

THE CLOCK TOWER HOUSE at 815 South Macomb Street was built a few years prior to his death in 1919 by Calvin C. Phillips, who is said to have designed buildings for the 1890 Paris World's Fair. The cottage resembled those of rural France and featured a square, medieval-looking clock tower. (Johnson)

SOME LANDMARKS AROUND
TOWN, some gone, some still standing:
Leon High School (*above*); First Baptist
Church, northwest corner College and
Adams (*right*); Masonic Building,
southwest corner of College and Adams
(*below right*); and Elks Club, east side of
Monroe between Call and Park, where
Leon County Library is now (*bottom*).

[93]

GOV. SIDNEY J. CATTS, a Baptist minister from DeFuniak Springs, becomes Florida's 22nd Governor on January 2, 1917, as he takes the oath of office in inaugural ceremonies at the Capitol. When he was a candidate for Governor, he told his listeners: "I know and you know that the pore man in Florida today has but three friends—Gawd Almighty, Sears Roebuck, and Sidney J. Catts." He was elected on a fluke. He had been counted out as the Democratic nominee after a hotly disputed primary vote. Then he got on the general election ballot as nominee for the Prohibition Party. He defeated W. V. Knott, the Democrats' standard-bearer, which was one of the few times in history that the Democratic nominee didn't go on to become Governor.

Tallahassee from 1920-1940

THE UNION BANK in the early 1920s. A man named William "Money" Williams came from North Carolina to Tallahassee about 1830 with a wagonload of money to start a bank. He built this little structure that served as a financial institution for many years. His charter was bought up by the Union Bank which was created in 1833 by the Territorial Council with John G. Gamble as president. The panic of 1837, costly Indian wars, a frost that destroyed citrus crops, and unsound banking practices led to the closing of the Union Bank in 1843. In 1973, the bank was moved to a prominent spot on U.S. highway 27, just east of the Capitol.

A FAMILIAR SIGHT around Tallahassee in the early 1920s was the late Hyman Myers, a fur trader, shown here with some coon skins and his Model T Ford. (Johnson)

A FAITHFUL SERVANT under many Florida governors as butler at the Governor's Mansion was Martin Van Buren Tanner. He began his notable career with the State on August 22, 1921, when Governor Hardee was in office. He was still active during the administration of Gov. Fuller Warren in the late 1940s and early 50s.

LAWYER AND BANKER from Live Oak, Cary A. Hardee, became Florida's 23rd Governor on January 4, 1921, in colorful inaugural ceremonies on the Capitol steps.

RASCAL YARD was what they called the Public Market on the west side of Adams at Jefferson (now the site of City Hall). This view to the southeast is from the corner of Jefferson and Duval, with the dome of the State Capitol in the background.

LEON COUNTY COURT HOUSE is shown after undergoing a remodeling in 1924.

UP-TO-DATE fire-fighting apparatus of the local Fire Department in 1924. The Department had three paid full-time men and 20 partially-paid volunteers. It boasted two triple-combination motor-driven pumpers carrying 12,000 feet of hose.

TEAMS OF OXEN were still a common mode of transportation, whether for deliveries such as wood for the fireplace (*above*), or just to get from here to there, as the old gentleman who moves along leisurely at Duval and College (*below*).

IN THE WAKE of the Florida real estate "boom" and the influx of tourists to the state, a widespread roadbuilding program took place. Here is the intersection of State Road No. 1 to Pensacola and No. 10 north to Atlanta in 1929.

THIS PRETTY BUILDING, at 727 South Calhoun St. photographed in 1929, was the Caroline Brevard Grammar School at the time. It served as a school for 35 years and was acquired by the State and renovated in 1959 for use as State offices. It's called the Bloxham building, in honor of Gov. William D. Bloxham, a native of Leon County, who served two terms as Governor (1881-85 and 1897-1901).

DALE MABRY FIELD, Tallahassee's fine new airport, was dedicated before a crowd of thousands on November 11-12, 1929. Vendors were on hand and the phrenology stand had a sign saying "Change sorrow to joy. Be master of your Destiny." The field was taken over by the U.S. Air Force during World War II and was redesignated Dale Mabry Field on August 25, 1941, after having been activated on January 21 of that year. Thousands of fighter pilots were trained here. One of the first groups of Chinese pilots underwent training at Dale Mabry in early 1942 as also did members of the famous 99th Fighter Squadron, black pilots under the command at the time of Lt. Col. Benjamin O. Davis, who later was to become a General.

[100]

THROUGH THE YEARS, this noble mansion "The Columns" has been a famous landmark in the capital city. This is how it looked in 1925 when Ford automobiles were filling the streets.

THE WAY IT LOOKED at Thomas Hayward's place at 216 South Adams Street in the 1930s.

WHERE THE PRINCE LAY IN STATE. This is the Gamble mansion at 202 W. College Avenue in 1934. Tradition says Prince Achille Murat lay in state here before his funeral.

TALLAHASSEE'S ATTRACTIVE POST OFFICE on the north side of Park between Monroe and Adams was constructed in 1935 and is still serving the public. It was the former site of the Leon County Court House and the Leon Hotel. Tallahassee's Post Office dates back to the Territorial days, having been established on May 13, 1825. Ambrose Crane was the first Postmaster.

MUNICIPAL EMPLOYEES in 1937: Police, Fire, Garbage, and Public Utilities.

THE MARTIN BUILDING on South
Adams Street between W. Jefferson and
W. Pensacola Streets, was built in 1927
and housed State offices. Later it was used
as City Hall. The building was named in
honor of Gov. John W. Martin who was
serving at the time the structure went up.
He was Governor from 1925 to 1929.

THE TOWN wasn't so built up in 1926
when this photo was taken of Florida
State College for Women campus. The
photo is actually a composite, with
Montgomery Gymnasium, built in 1938,
having been added, somewhat askew.

[104]

A SIGNIFICANT OCCASION was the first scheduled flight of Eastern Air Lines through Tallahassee on October 10, 1938. Among those taking part in the festivities were Tallahassee Mayor J. R. Jinks, second from left; Capt. Eddie V. Rickenbacker, president of Eastern Air Lines, fourth from left, and H. P. Ford, Tallahassee City Manager, eighth from left.

THE OLD SEARS BUILDING at the corner of Monroe and Jefferson housed the department store for 30 years. Before the turn of the century, the building was the home of a cigar factory. It closed down in 1904 because Leon County was voted dry and the Latin cigarmakers wouldn't stay in a town without liquor, beer, or wine. (Johnson)

Tallahassee since 1940

FLORIDA'S OLDEST ANNUAL CELEBRATION is the May Day Party under the 200-year-old May Oak on Lewis Green on Park Avenue. Ever since 1833 the townspeople have followed the charming old English custom of welcoming in the May with a festival for children. World War II had its effect on May Day. In 1942, the first May Day after Pearl Harbor, a Pan-American theme was carried out by the Leon High School Glee Club's rendition of Spanish-American song hits and the rhumba, tango, and conga. The next year it was "May Day—The United Nations Way." The band opened with songs of several of our Allies, the Glee Club sang "Dark Eyes" as a tribute to Russia, and performers entertained the court with a Chinese dance, an Indian dance, the Czechoslovakian polka, and a rhumba. The traditional May Pole dance concluded the program. The highly popular social event has had various sponsors through the years and presently is promoted by the Tallahassee Society of the Sons of the American Revolution. The venerable old May Oak recently was evaluated by Charles E. Salter of the State Division of Forestry—who appraised it at $33,637.

POET ROBERT FROST was a distinguished visitor to the campus of Florida State College for Women in the early 1940s. He's shown chatting with a couple of coeds.

GOODBYE CONES, HELLO HOLLANDS. The outgoing and incoming Governors and First Ladies pose for the press on Inauguration Day in 1941. Left to right Mrs. Fred P. Cone, outgoing First Lady; Mrs. Spessard L. Holland, incoming First Lady; outgoing Gov. Fred P. Cone, a Lake City banker, and incoming Gov. Spessard L. Holland, a Bartow lawyer.

THE JUNIOR WOMAN'S CLUB has been a lively and effective civic organization in Tallahassee for many years. Here's a good look at the head table at a function in December, 1944.

DURING WORLD WAR II there were thousands of young airmen stationed at Dale Mabry Field in Tallahassee. Young ladies of the city formed the Junior Hostess Club and sponsored dances. Some of the hostesses and guests rallied around the punch bowl for a picture in February, 1945.

FRATERNAL LODGES have played a large role in the life of the community. One of the oldest and largest is the Elks Club. This photo was taken at an Elks function in April, 1945.

WORLD WAR II IS OVER! It's V-J Day, August 15, 1945, and Tallahassee, along with the rest of the Allied world, pulled out all stops to celebrate victory. Crowds packed the sidewalks of Monroe Street to see a hastily-organized parade march by. It was truly a joyous occasion.

BY NOVEMBER, 1945, young veterans of World War II had joined their older comrades from World War I in the American Legion.

IT WAS GRADUATION DAY 1946 at Florida State College for Women, and the processional was on. Students and faculty march into historic Westcott Hall, one of the oldest buildings on the campus, a landmark since its completion in 1910. James Diament Westcott Jr., born in 1802, gave his name to the famous old building atop College Avenue. He lived briefly in Florida, became one of its first U.S. Senators for less than four years, moved to New York in 1850, died in Montreal, and was buried in Tallahassee in 1880. In 1947 F.S.C.W. became Florida State University—and co-educational. In 1969, Westcott Hall was struck by fire which seriously damaged the old structure.

TRAFFIC WAS PICKING UP, but Tallahassee was still a rather peaceful town in 1946. This is looking South on Adams Street at College Ave. (Johnson)

IT WAS A QUIET DAY IN 1948 when this photograph of South Monroe Street was made. The Capitol dome looms large in the background. There have been many changes in this stretch of the street since.

"KEEP AMERICA UNCONQUERED" was the theme the armed forces recruiters used in an exhibit at the Ritz Theatre on September 22, 1948, when the movie, "Unconquered," starring Gary Cooper and Paulette Goddard, was showing.

A TRANQUIL SCENE in the capital city's residential section in 1948. The canopy of ancient live oaks adds to the peacefulness.

[114]

CAME THE FLOODS in 1948, and streets in Tallahassee were covered with water.

TUNG ORCHARD in Tallahassee in 1948 (*above*). This tree, a native of China where it is cultivated commercially for thousands of years, produces a nut-like seed from which Tung Oil, the world's quickest-drying paint oil, is extracted in several modern Tung mills in Florida. The first tree in Florida was planted in Tallahassee in 1906, and half a century later some 40,000 acres were under cultivation. Leon County growers are checking the quality of the crop (*right*).

WOMEN CELEBRITIES visit Tallahassee. At an autograph party, famed author Marjorie Kinnan Rawlings signs copies of her "The Yearling" for Mrs. Frank D. Moor and her two children, Bettie Bedell and Bill Moor. Miss Rawlings did her best writing in a rural Florida setting at her home in Cross Creek, near Gainesville. Mrs. Eleanor Roosevelt, wife of President Franklin D. Roosevelt, was a visitor to Florida's capital city, and is seen here with Mrs. Frank Moor and Mrs. Sara Pepper Willis.

BURSTING WITH PRIDE, newly inaugurated Gov. Fuller Warren cuts the cake at a celebration on his Inauguration Day in January, 1949.

THE INAUGURAL PARADE down Adams Street greeted Gov. Fuller Warren in January, 1949. The old Union Bank is seen at left (it's been moved to Apalachee Parkway near the Capitol); "The Columns," a mansion of the Territorial days was a popular restaurant called The Dutch Kitchen in 1949 which was moved in recent years a few blocks and became headquarters for the Tallahassee Chamber of Commerce; and the ancient First Presbyterian Church.

[117]

A MANSION dating back to 1888 serves as the official residence for the President of Florida State University. The white-columned residence was built that year for the W. M. McIntosh family on the site now occupied by the Supreme Court building. In the late 1940s, it was cut in half and moved in halves to its present site at 1030 West Tennessee Street, just before this photograph was made.

A LARGE ELECTRIC POWER DAM in Florida is located on Lake Talquin near Tallahassee.

THE DUKE AND DUCHESS OF WINDSOR were occasional visitors to Tallahassee in the early 1950s. They stayed with their friend, Mrs. George F. Baker, at her Horseshoe Plantation in North Leon County. Editor Malcolm Johnson of the *Tallahassee Democrat* reported that the Duchess, one of the world's best-dressed women, habituee of the finest shops in Paris and the rest of the world, said she always enjoyed shopping in Tallahassee!

"IKE AND MAMIE" arrive at Tallahassee airport during the 1952 campaign when Gen. Dwight D. Eisenhower was seeking the Presidency. John Eisenhower is walking beside his father.

CHRISTMAS 1948 on Monroe Street showed that traffic had picked up—not only because of Christmas shoppers, but also because of the steady increase in numbers of automobiles.

THE ANNUAL WILLIAMS FAMILY REUNION is one of the most popular events in North Florida, a "happening" of significance for over 70 years. The saga of the Williams family began in the 1630s when the family sailed from England. Eventually three of the brothers settled in West Florida. The reunion is that of the descendants of Andrew Elton Williams, who settled in Florida in 1822, became a cattleman, married twice, and sired 23 children. The Williams clan now numbers more than 25,000 members in Florida, and another 25,000 throughout the world. One of the two men selected to locate a site for the capital was John Lee Williams of Pensacola, who also recommended the name of Tallahassee. Through the years, members of the family have been active in politics. More than 2,000 persons turn up for the reunion dinner-on-the-ground, and food is served "by the ton" on the long table.

THE OLD GRIST MILL was still grinding away in the 1950s at Sheppard's Grist Mill.

ANOTHER RURAL ACTIVITY in Leon County was the naval stores and Boynton's turpentine still.

HANDSOME DAN McCARTY of Fort Pierce was inaugurated as Florida's 31st Govenor on January 6, 1953. He's being sworn in by Justice H. L. (Tom) Sebring of the Florida Supreme Court. Standing behind them are Secretary of State R. A. Gray and Supreme Court Clerk Guyte P. McCord.

193
THE DAN McCARTY INAUGURATION was the first held on the West side of the Capitol in what was then called Waller Park, honoring Judge Curtis L. Waller of the U.S. Circuit Court of Appeals, a Tallahassean. The new State Capitol is being constructed on this site in 1974.

GOVERNOR McCARTY WAS FELLED by a heart attack on February 25, 1953, and was unable to appear before the Legislature at its joint session in April. Secretary of State R. A. Gray read the Governor's Message. In front of the rostrum were Gray's colleagues on the State Cabinet.

THE HOUSE OF REPRESENTATIVES in session on April 22, 1953. Speaker presiding was Farris Bryant, who was to serve as governor from 1961 to 1964. Prior to the 1961 session, members of the House did not have private offices. The only available place for them to work was at their desks in the Chamber, hence the necessity for secretaries to sit on the House floor. The open galleries were necessary because of the lack of a public address system. The office of the Speaker, that of the Clerk, and the Enrolling and Engrossing room were located in the east area, access to which could be gained only through the House Chamber. The almost steady stream of employees going back and forth through the Chamber added confusion to an already congested situation.

THE SABAL PALM, also known as cabbage palm is Florida's official State Tree. What might be considered the "official" State Tree is a thriving sabal palmetto on the Capitol grounds. A marker at the foot is dedicated to the memory of Gov. Dan McCarty, who signed the bill designating the Sabal Palmetto as Florida State Tree on June 11, 1953, shortly before his death. The sabal palm grows all over the state. The State seal, which was designed in 1868, features a stately sabal. (Dunn)

SIX FLORIDA GOVERNORS and one from Georgia at a party given by Fred Mahan, prominent Monticello nurseryman, on May 7, 1953. Left to right are George A. Smathers, U.S. Senator for many years; Gov. LeRoy Collins (1955-61); Gov. Doyle E. Carlton (1929-33); Gov. Cary A. Hardee (1921-25); Fred Mahan; Gov. Fuller Warren (1949-53); Gov. Marvin Griffin of Georgia; Gov. Spessard L. Holland (1941-45), who also was a U.S. Senator many years, and Gov. Millard F. Caldwell (1945-49).

AREN'T THEY BEAUTIFUL? Lovely ladies pose prettily for the camera during the May Day celebration in 1955.

Facing page: FOR THREE DECADES, a New York millionaire, Alfred B. Maclay, developed his Tallahassee hillside home into one of the South's finest azalea and camellia collections. He purchased the property five and a half miles north of Tallahassee on U.S. 319 in 1923. He called his plantation "Killearn" for a little village in Scotland, the birthplace of his great grand-father. In 1953, after Maclay's death, his family gave the fabulous gardens to the State of Florida for a park. In 1965, the park's name was changed to the Alfred B. Maclay Gardens. Among the more famous of varieties of camellia at the garden is the Aunt Jetty. It was brought from Baltimore in the 1860s by Angelica Robinson, who was known as Aunt Jetty. She became the bride of pioneer Robert Howard Gamble. It was the first camellia to be planted at Maclay. (Dunn)

A STADIUM FOR FLORIDA STATE (*below*) was dedicated in 1953 and honored Dr. Doak S. Campbell, veteran president of the institution. The Jaycees backed FSU stadium with a $50,000 check (*right*). Edwin M. Clark, seated right, Tallahassee Junior Chamber of Commerce, hands the check to Dr. Doak S. Campbell, FSU president. Standing, left to right, are J. Kenneth Ballinger, Tallahassee attorney and general chairman of the ticket sales campaign, and Rainey Cawthon, ticket sales chairman.

"JAKE" GAITHER, the famous and popular coach of Florida A. & M. for many years leads his football charges in prayer.

FOR MANY YEARS, the Florida Supreme Court held sessions in this building (*left*). It was replaced in 1948 with a magnificent new building, photographed shortly after its official dedication on December 29, 1948. In front is Waller Park.

HE STOOD TALL in Florida politics, did William V. Knott, who was born in 1863 and died in 1965. He came close to being elected Governor of Florida in the hot campaign of 1916. He was the Democratic nominee, ekeing out a win over Sidney J. Catts, but Catts came back in the general election as the Prohibition Party nominee and beat Knott. The distinguished centenarian had served as State Comptroller, State Treasurer, and State Auditor. He is the father of Circuit Judge James R. Knott of West Palm Beach, a past president of the Florida Historical Society. This photo of W. V. Knott was taken in his later years by Red Kerce, photographer for the *Tallahassee Democrat*.

THE FLORIDA SUPREME COURT in 1954: (left to right, seated) H. L. (Tom) Sebring, Glenn Terrell, B. K. Roberts and Elwyn Thomas, and (standing) John E. Mathews, T. Frank Hobson, and E. Harris Drew.

[133]

THE 'STATE SHACK' is what Gov. Fuller Warren called the old Governor's Mansion, built in 1906, when he asked that a new official residence be constructed. The new mansion was finsihed during the administration of Gov. LeRoy Collins. Before demolishing the old mansion, an auction was held in 1955 (*above*), and the building was then razed (*below*).

AN OUTSTANDING EDIFICE in downtown Tallahassee is the handsome First Baptist Church.

AN AERIAL VIEW of the widespread campus of Florida Agricultural & Mechanical University a few years after it was designated a University in 1953.

AS LATE AS THE 1950s, the hooded members of the Ku Klux Klan burned crosses and demonstrated in Tallahassee. During his administration, Gov. Fuller Warren referred to the Klansmen as "hooded jerks."

The Tallahassee Democrat newspaper observed its fiftieth anniversary in 1955. In photo are Mrs. Lilias Collins Edmonds, daughter of John G. Collins, founder; Col. Lloyd C. Griscom, then the owner, and Mrs. Milton A. Smith, widow of former owner. *The Democrat* was founded as *The Weekly True Democrat* by John G. Collins, March 3, 1905. Milton A. Smith purchased the newspaper in 1908. On April 6, 1915, he made it *The Daily Democrat*. Lloyd G. Griscom became owner in 1929. It was purchased by Knight Newspapers, Inc., on March 1, 1965. Vol. 1, No. 1 of *The True Democrat* explained the name showed dedication to "true and tried doctrines of The Old Time Democracy . . . as distinguished from . . . mischievous . . . fads and fallacies of the day."

SNOW IN TALLAHASSEE! The solid snowfall in 1958 was unusual. It covered the new Executive Mansion and the surrounding grounds (*below*), but the inhabitants made the best of it. Mary Call and Darby Collins (*left*), daughters of then-governor LeRoy Collins, are busily at work building a snowman.

THE DIXIE HOTEL across Monroe Street from the State Capitol for many years was a landmark and popular gathering spot for politicians, lobbyists, and other visitors to Tallahassee.

Following page: GOOD NIGHT FROM THE STATE CAPITOL of Florida. The old building, ready for occupancy when Florida became a state in 1845, has watched over the capital city of Tallahassee all these years. (Dunn)